THE PHILOSOPHY OF JESUS

Other Newt List books by Ernest Holmes

Creative Mind

Creative Mind and Success

Ernest Holmes Speaks

How to Use Your Power:
20 Practical Lessons for Creating A Balanced Life

Life Is What You Make It

60 Meditations for a Mindful Life

The Basics of Spiritual Mind Healing

The Bible in Light of Spiritual Philosophy

The Meaning of the Bible

The Philosophy of Emerson

The Power of This Thing Called Life

THE PHILOSOPHY OF JESUS

UPDATED AND GENDER-NEUTRAL

ERNEST HOLMES

newt
LIST

A Newt List Publication
Chicago • New York

CONTENTS

THE PHILOSOPHY
OF JESUS

CHAPTER 1

THE POWER
THAT JESUS USED

THROUGHOUT OUR LIVES, PEOPLE AROUND THE WORLD have read and wondered about the miracles of Jesus. But to how many of them has come the thought that this same power must be available to everyone? We are so much accustomed to thinking of Jesus as a man filled with love and compassion and human kindness that we have overlooked something else about him that is equally important. Jesus had access to a spiritual power that he used in every way. To him, it seemed the most natural thing in the world that he should be able to tell the paralyzed to walk, multiply the loaves and fishes, or still the wind and waves.

What we want to find out, then, is the nature of this

power that Jesus used, learn how it operates, and apply it in our own lives in helping ourselves and others. This does not necessarily refer to the healing miracles, when people were restored to physical health. While this is wonderful and good, there is much more to life than merely getting rid of pain. Jesus had access to some kind of power that was available for every purpose. He had access to an intelligence that guided him in everything he did. And he had a deep, inward peace and feeling of security that removed all confusion, doubt and uncertainty from his mind.

We want to find the key that unlocks the doorway to the power greater than we are. We want to discover the secret that Jesus so plainly told us was inherent in the kind of relationship he had with God, who is present everywhere and in everyone.

This field of science is devoted to the discovery of the powers and energies in nature and learning how to apply them to our everyday needs. These powers, uncovered by science, have always existed. They were always there, waiting to be used, and are always ready to respond when we use them rightly.

We think of scientists as professionals who use the power of nature. We do not say that they possess it as a personal thing, because, of course, this would not be true. What we say is that science discovers the power, unlocks its energy, and uses it for definite purposes for the betterment of humanity. What we really mean by this is that there are certain physical laws and physical powers in nature that are greater than we are, but that can be used, and that these powers operate for us as though they were our servants. We employ them; we do not implore them. That is, we do not beseech them, we do not coerce them, and, as a matter of fact, we do not even concentrate them. We merely use them.

But Jesus had access to another kind of power, which he called the power of the Spirit. We cannot doubt that there are spiritual powers that act like physical ones, that act for us and, in a certain sense, become our servants when we learn how they operate. In dealing with these powers, we must always comply with them, because the secrets of nature are disclosed and the powers of nature can be used only when we first comply with the way they work. Of all people in the world, scientists are the most humble. They stand in reverence and awe before the wonders of a self-operating universe that operates independently of our will, our coercion, or even our desire.

When it was discovered that hens lay eggs, sit on them, and hatch out chicks, someone had the foresight to realize that you can make as many hens as you want sit on as many eggs as they can cover and they will produce as many chickens as are desirable, provided you actually put the hens and the eggs together. This is an example of the way nature works, with complete independence of our thoughts, will, and desires, but always with this in mind, that when we comply with the way it works we receive the benefit.

It is the same with every scientific discovery. In the laboratory, scientists observe the laws of nature, discover how they work, and then apply them. Nature itself produces the result. We are so used to this that we take it for granted, not realizing that new things are being revealed to us every day because we are learning how to cooperate with the source of all power.

Jesus understood a different set of laws, and because he used these laws a power was delivered to him that has amazed the world. It is our purpose to rediscover these laws, find out how they work, apply them for every legitimate purpose, and then reap the benefit. In doing this, it is necessary that we follow the example of the one who really knew. The only reason we know that Jesus really knew is that he proved his claim. What we should do, then, is to find out exactly what Jesus believed and why and how he used this secret of the ages so effectively.

The first thing to learn is that Jesus believed himself to be one with God, and he believed that the divine presence was right where he was. He communed with this presence through prayers and meditation until it was the most real thing to him in life. We find, then, that the whole background of his teaching starts with the idea that there is such a presence and such a power, that the presence is accessible to all of us, and that the power can be used by anyone who has faith in it.

This is no doubt the greatest secret of the ages. It is the miracle of the answer to prayer. It is the miracle of life itself. We need to believe that you and I, so little and so alone, have access to a power that has the possibility of making everything in our lives happy and harmonious if we cooperate with it. So how can we believe in a power that we can neither touch nor taste nor handle?

The answer to this is simple enough. Let us go back to the hens sitting on their eggs. Neither you nor I nor the hen ever put a chicken in an egg, nor did we ever take one out. The hen, instinctively, by some method of which she is not consciously aware, follows the law of her own life. She lays the eggs and sits on them and nature performs the miracle for her. The power that does this cannot be touched, tasted or handled. It cannot be seen. Yet we are so used to it that we never question the results. We build incubators, set eggs in them and subject them to a certain heat for a certain period of time with complete assurance and absolute faith, because experience has taught us that we can do this and chicks will hatch.

So it is with every law that we use. No one has ever seen the powers of nature. We only see how they work and we accept them with the simplicity of a child. How can we believe in a divine presence when we have not seen it? The answer to this is simple. How can we believe in a law of attraction and repulsion that we have not seen? How can we believe that a magnet will attract iron, since we do not see the power of attraction that draws it? No one has ever seen love or human affection. No one has seen kindness, tolerance or human understanding, but we have felt them, and we have no more doubt of their existence than we do of our own being.

I do not think we need to be concerned with the fact that we do not see God other than in God's creation, or that we have not seen the forces of nature other than in and through what they do. When Jesus told us that we should have faith, he was not telling us about something that is impossible for us attain. Jesus was the most simple and direct of all people. He knew that faith is a natural attitude of mind. It is the very simplicity of his teaching that eludes us. As a matter of fact, it is so easy that it is hard, so simple that it is difficult, so direct that we fail to catch its significance. Whether or not we know it, we all have faith, but we are mostly using it in reverse.

Jesus told us that there is a divine presence that will guide us if we let it. He told us that there is a power that will operate for us if we believe that it will. But he also told us that this presence is love and this power is good, and that we cannot hope to derive the greatest benefit from the presence as divine guidance or the power as the operation of divine love until we first greet the presence in love and use the power for good. Jesus laid down no instruction other than this: God is love and God is good. It follows that divine power is delivered to us only in such degree as we love and are constructive.

All the prayers and willpower of humankind can neither add to nor subtract from the powers of nature. This is so self-evident that one cannot even argue against it. What we have to do, then, is invite the presence and use the power. We invite the divine presence every time we think about it in love and with true humility. We draw inspiration into our minds and our imaginations and release it through our actions when we recognize this presence, and we benefit from the use of the power when we comply with the way it works.

Here is where our great experiment in using the power that Jesus understood starts. This is the very beginning of it. We must believe that there is a divine presence. Of course, our belief does not create it; it merely acknowledges it. It is this acknowledgment of the divine presence that Jesus was referring to when he said, "Your Creator knows what things you have need of before you ask."

Artists believe in the presence of beauty. They invite it into their thoughts, wills, and imaginations. They make themselves open to it. Our acknowledgement of the presence of God should be as simple as this and as direct. No matter what we are doing, we should start with this basic thought:

"God is all there is. God is right where I am. Divine

intelligence is now directing me. I not only invite it but I believe it is here. There is nothing in me that can deny me the privilege of receiving this divine guidance. There is something in me that knows what to do under every circumstance. It knows how to meet every situation and knows how to overcome every obstacle. I am in partnership with the infinite Mind that creates everything and sustains everything. I am one with God."

We should entertain thoughts like these until they become habitual, that is, until nothing in us denies them. It is not going to take any more faith than we now have, because one of the greatest lessons we can learn about faith is that we always possess it. Too often, though, we use it negatively. In truth, we are always affirming something, be it for good or ill. We are always saying either "I can" or "I cannot." What we need to do is eliminate the negative and accentuate the positive. In doing this we gradually acquire the habit of affirmative thinking.

In addition to this belief—that there is a divine presence guiding and leading us gently but certainly on the pathway to success, happiness, and wholeness—we must also come to believe that there is a power that always accompanies this recognition of the divine presence. We must have faith that this power operates on our word. We do not see its operation. We do not touch it or taste it or handle it. But we can feel it. It is this deep, underlying conviction and feeling that we must acquire.

This is not difficult. It is merely a question of training the mind to believe in and understand spiritual law in the same manner that it believes in and understands the operation of physical law. If it were something too difficult, then it would be beyond our reach and we would become discouraged even before we started. The whole thing has to be kept simple, direct and sincere. The power that Jesus used was a spiritual power. He knew that it operated on and through his word of faith, and he had such complete reliance on it that he did not hesitate to tell the paralyzed to get up and walk.

It is not the words Jesus used which performed the miracle. It was his inner conviction of the power that operated on, in and through his words. He called this *faith and belief* and, in doing so, reduced it to a mental attitude or a way of thinking that we can all understand. There is something that operates on our belief and acts exactly like a law because it *is* a law and tends to bring about conditions that correspond to our faith, our belief and our way of thinking.

Frequently, when we begin to use this power consciously, we find that our thoughts are unruly. In one moment we affirm some good that we desire, and in the very next moment we deny what we have affirmed. In this way we build a mental house divided against itself. We may as well recognize this fact because it is an important one. But in recognizing it there is no occasion to

despair, because we know that thinking is really a movement of the mind on itself, right where we are. We are
the thinker; therefore we can change our thoughts.

This is why Jesus told us that sometimes only prayer
and fasting can bring about the desired result. He did not
mean that God listens when we do a lot of talking. What
he meant was that we should pray affirmatively and we
should fast when it comes to negative thinking. This is
the sacrifice we make when we surrender our doubts and
fears to the great affirmations of life. To "pray without
ceasing" means to continue in an affirmative attitude of
mind, and "fasting" means to refrain from all negative
thoughts and ideas.

There must come a new impulse to the mind, a new
way of looking at things. This is what Jesus called the new
birth. He referred to this when he said that we must be
born again. We must be born of the Spirit, which means
being born into a complete conviction of the presence,
power and activity of God in and through us. The results
that follow this new birth are automatic. This is why Jesus
told us that if we seek the realm of God first, everything
else will be added.

What a wonderful adventure lies before us! How
grateful we should be for the opportunity to live, love,
work and play. We should have a keen sense of anticipation and enthusiasm, because we know that we are working with a spiritual power greater than we are, a law of

Mind that is available to create every good thing in life. I believe this is the secret to the power Jesus demonstrated, as well as to the understanding of his teachings. We may call this *faith*, we may call it *religion* or we may call it *worship*. It is all these and more. Yet it resolves itself into a simple, sincere and direct approach to God and to the law of Mind.

The world is searching for the answers to its problems. Frustrated and distraught, disillusioned and chagrined, it stands on the brink of two possibilities: to be, or not to be. Our world is shocked by the realization of what it has brought on itself. Nothing is more certain than that we have failed. As never before, millions of people are ready to try something else, something that for far too long has been neglected and something that can make it whole. It is clear that we must rediscover the secret of the ages and come into close cooperation with the presence that made us and the power that sustains us. Along this pathway lies the hope of humanity. This, and this only, is the road to peace, prosperity and happiness.

CHAPTER 2

ONE INDIVIDUAL
WITH GOD

IN ALL THE YEARS OF WORKING WITH PEOPLE, I HAVE
never found anyone who did not secretly long to find
something that would make them whole and happy,
something that would give them a sense of security and
safety. I have never found an individual who did not
wish the same good for others. I am a great believer
in the innate goodness of people, and I know through
much experience that the average person wants to do
the best they can.

I have frequently asked people, "Why don't you learn
to use spiritual power so that it will be effective in your
life and in the lives of those around you?" They usually
answer, "I don't know how" or "I haven't the faith" or

"I haven't the training or the education" or "I haven't the opportunity."

They probably use these alibis because it does not occur to them that they have to start right where they are and use such faith as they possess to acquire more through actual experience.

Jesus set about to definitely prove what one person with God could do. He demonstrated for all ages that just one person with implicit faith can do anything. If there is any one fact that Jesus emphasized beyond all others it was that what he was doing others could do also if they believed they could and if they believed in God.

Jesus knew that one person with God is a majority. As we look back over his life and rethink its meaning, we discover that he had trained himself to believe in God. To him, the presence of God was as real as sunshine, as distinct as the wind blowing. So great was his concept of the power of God that he said that heaven and earth would pass away, but his words would remain until all is fulfilled.

This, then, is the kind of faith we are called on to have. It is not a faith that is found in books. It is not a faith that someone else can give to us, because no one can possibly give us that which we already possess. Rather, it is something we now have but have not been using, and we have not been using it because we have not recognized that it is already right where we are.

One person with God is a wonderful idea, and it will

be even more wonderful when we realize that that one person is our self. But that one person is not our self unless we include God. It is one person *with God* that we must emphasize.

God exists everywhere, and in God we live, move and have our being. The Spirit is within us as well as around us, and we can have no life apart from it. All the life of the Spirit, then, belongs to each one of us, but, in a certain sense, we only have as much as we use. Again, as we reflect on the life and teaching of Jesus, we find that he spent much time alone communing with God. In his instructions he tells us that the power of God acts independently of any circumstance because it *creates* circumstances. When we get lost in the circumstances that surround us and become confused over them, and when we feel isolated and alone, then the struggle for existence becomes unbearable and we feel that the odds are against us. This is why Jesus told us not to judge according to the appearance, but to judge righteously. That is, we should not look at the obstruction in our lives and say it is too great to overcome. We should know that even in the obstruction that confronts us, at the very center of it, there is a power that can resolve all obstacles, solve all problems and meet every emergency.

It becomes a question of whether our faith is greater than the obstruction, whether we are becoming confused over conditions or thinking peacefully and calmly about them. When it comes right down to it, the only choice is whether we believe in a power greater than we are that we can use, or whether we actually believe that this power is ready, willing and able to respond to us.

Jesus said, "It is your Creator's good pleasure to give you the domain." Life has made the gift, but we must accept it. Jesus, being human, may have been filled with many doubts, particularly in the beginning of his ministry. Imagine Jesus standing in the midst of a multitude that was clamoring for healing—bringing their sick, lame and blind to him—looking out over this vast sea of faces. Perhaps the question came to him: "Can I make these people whole?"

We know what his answer was, because he said, "I can of my own self do nothing…but the Spirit that dwells in me, it does the work." We can almost sense the triumphant concept in his consciousness. One person with God is supreme. Jesus, as a human being, had no power of himself at all, but all power was given to him in heaven and on earth because he had acquired all love and had become intimate with the divine presence that flows through everything.

The power that Jesus manifested was divine. It was not his will but his willingness to believe that gave him power. It was not a concentration of spiritual forces that Jesus exercised, but rather a childlike and implicit faith in the reality of the Spirit in human affairs.

One of the most amazing things about Jesus was that he never tried to influence anyone. He was not at all like those people who have developed such terrific personalities that their influence dominates others. This is exactly what Jesus did not do and warned us against doing. Quite the reverse, Jesus said that the realm of God is like a child. It is simplicity and sincerity. It is quiet acceptance rather than loud proclamation.

With this in mind, let us think of Jesus feeding the multitude. His disciples had asked him to disperse the crowd so that they might go home where there would be food for them. But Jesus turned to his disciples and asked why they did not feed the multitude. They replied that they had nothing with which to feed them. "There is a child here who has five barley loaves and two small fishes, but what are they among so many?"

Perhaps here is one of the greatest lessons in spiritual history. Jesus must have been surrounded by people of great knowledge. There were the doctors of law who thought they knew all the answers, trying to catch Jesus in a trap. There were his own followers who, although they had seen many miracles, could not believe that Jesus was able to feed the multitude out of nothing. And there was a young child with a few loaves and fishes, eager and expectant, holding out a meager fare to the hands of Jesus, who took the loaves and fishes, gave thanks, and distributed them to the multitude.

Let us think of this not only as an actual but also as a symbol of ourselves. There is a little child in each one of us. There is a hope and an inward spiritual realization in everyone, something that is beyond all doubt, fear and uncertainty. We would not be here if this were not true.

Let us think of this as a beautiful symbol: the intellect and the human will surrendering itself to some inward feeling, some childlike simplicity, some spontaneous joy, some complete faith. That child is in you and in me, and experience has never completely dimmed its vision. It is the childlike Spirit within us that we must cultivate because the child within us knows a language that the intellect has failed to learn.

Let us think of Jesus standing before the tomb of Lazarus, where friends and relatives had gathered hoping to find some comfort from his words, but not even daring to dream that Lazarus could be resurrected from the dead. Jesus stood there in front of the tomb—one individual alone with God. He stood just a little apart from the others and lifted up his soul in silent communication with the Spirit of all life, the Spirit that knows no death. Something flowed into him, and he turned around and said, "Take away the stone." But they argued that Lazarus had been dead for four days and they dare not roll away the stone.

Now watch carefully what Jesus did and listen to his words as he said, "Lord, I thank you that you have heard me. And I know that you hear me always." This is recognition of the divine presence and the divine power that is always available. Here is faith and unification. There was no doubt, no uncertainty, no stammering or stuttering, no imploring or beseeching. Just the simple words: "I thank you (gratitude) that you hear me always (certainty)."

Next comes the supreme command: "Lazarus, come forth." One individual with God, recognizing life instead of death, until the tomb surrendered its dead and Lazarus came forth, and Jesus told them to "loose him and let him go."

Lazarus is each one of us, bound by the restriction of circumstances, tied by the habits of thought and incarcerated in a tomb from which it seems as though we cannot extricate ourselves. "Loose him, and let him go." There is much in each one of us that must be loosed: the ropes of fear that bind us; the winding sheet of doubt and uncertainty; the darkness and gloom of our self-imposed prison; and the stone that must be rolled away. Yes, and the doubt of others who would block the action of faith because all they see is the stone, the tomb and the dead person inside, and they say, "You dare not roll away the stone."

Let us think of the silent communion we have with the Spirit that knows no bondage, with the life that knows no death, and with the power that knows no obstruction.

As we do this, something within us comes alive and gives us the courage and assurance to say, "Lord, I thank you that you have heard me, and I know that you hear me always." Out of this communion comes a divine authority, which is the gift of heaven.

One with God. You are that one, and I am that one. Only one, because in the silent inward precinct of our own minds, no one enters but ourselves. Something within stands halfway between heaven and earth: the child who is not afraid and the person of wisdom who has overcome fear. There is one side of us that has never entered the shadow of doubt. This is what we must develop if we are to prove that one person with God can be supreme in whatever is right, just or true. Just one person with God.

CHAPTER 3

THE SCIENCE OF PRAYER

ONE OF THE OUTSTANDING THINGS ABOUT JESUS WAS THAT he did not reserve the use of spiritual power for some future event, but boldly proclaimed that the realm of God is here and now and that the law of Mind is available for every legitimate and constructive human purpose. Jesus said that whatever things we desire when we pray, we should believe that we have them. He said that unless our prayers are amiss, that is, unless they are contrary to good, they will be answered.

Jesus healed the sick, and yet one of his immediate followers was a physician. I think one of the things the world should be experimenting with more is exactly what Dr. Robert A. Millikan suggested: combining religion, faith and prayer with all the wonderful things now being worked out in the field of medicine. I believe that when we combine psychosomatic medicine, which is body-mind relationships, with spiritual power, we will have gone a long way toward finding the road to health. Most physicians prefer patients who have faith, and the more observing doctors prefer a household of faith surrounding their patients.

Jesus, in many ways, demonstrated the availability of the law of Mind to meet human needs wherever and whenever they arose. Perhaps we have fallen into the mistake of thinking that the law is available for only a few purposes. We should use spiritual power in everything we do, and we should have such a complete evidence that this power actually exists that there will be no question about it in our minds. Jesus said, "These signs shall follow them that believe." Taking his teaching as the great example, we should expect signs following our prayers of faith.

The question then arises: If there is such a power, why is it that our prayers are not answered? Many sincere people believe that God answers only certain prayers and not others. But another smaller group believes that all prayers will be answered when we pray correctly.

It was this latter position that Jesus took. He very carefully explained what he meant by right prayer. Right prayer, according to his teaching, includes the good of the other person as well as ourselves. For instance, he said that we should love our neighbor as we love ourselves. But in saying this, we should carefully note that Jesus did not say we must hate ourselves in order to love our neighbors. He knew that we are all important to God. We should love ourselves for what we really are and we should love our neighbors for what they really are. We should wish to do good to others, and we should desire that good will be done to us.

I believe that we pray correctly when there is nothing in our prayers that would hurt anyone. I believe we pray correctly when we pray unselfishly. This does not mean that we should exclude ourselves. It does mean that we should include others. Then, surely our prayers will be in accord with divine love and wisdom.

What can we do with this spiritual power that is closer to us than our very breath? How will we so attune ourselves to it that good will flow out in all directions and return to us hundredfold? We must first come to believe that there actually is such a power and that we can really use it.

We believe that there is a law of gravity that holds us where we place ourselves, and we have implicit faith in this law. We have faith in it and we are so accustomed to the idea that we never question it. This is the first requirement of the teaching of Jesus: *We must believe.* We must think of spiritual power, then, as a natural law, and think of faith and prayer as the right ways to use this law. Prayer is our communion with the Spirit, and faith is our definite acceptance that, through this communion, the law of Mind reacts to us and to others according to our belief.

Here is where religion, faith, prayer, and science combine. Communion with the divine presence helps us to arrive at the place of faith and acceptance, and it is this faith and acceptance that make prayer powerful.

You might ask, "Why can't I have the faith without the communion?" My answer would be another question: Can artists paint beautiful pictures unless they commune with beauty? God is peace, God is love, God is life and God is beauty. When we become peaceful and commune with this life, love, and beauty, something happens to us inside. It is as though a great power were flowing into us. So if someone were to ask, "Why can't we have faith without communion?" my answer would be, "It is communion that gives us faith."

The next step is to make God real to our own mind. This is something we each have to work out for ourselves. God is love; therefore, we should open up our minds to love. God is peace; therefore, we should become receptive to peace. God is good; therefore, we should meditate on goodness. When we sit quietly by ourselves and think of God as very close to us, and think of love and peace and goodness as the great reality, a surge of faith uplifts our mind.

Now we are ready to pray effectively, which merely means we are ready to make our spiritual affirmations with complete conviction because we know that we are dealing with a power greater than we are, a power that we do not coerce, coax or intrigue, because it is already here. It is right where we are. This power apparently flows through our words and is a divine law that always tends to produce the good we have accepted.

We should train our minds to think affirmatively. This means that we must winnow out all negations. We must dispel the darkness of doubt and fear. We could not do this if we felt we were depending on our own personal power any more than we believe we could use any other law in nature through exercising willpower or coercion.

When we pray affirmatively, we get results. We must train ourselves to expect definite results when we use spiritual power. This is done through what is called *meditation,* or *affirmative prayer.* We start with the thought that God is all there is. "There is one life, that life is God, that life is my life now." If we are praying for physical wellbeing, we might say, "There is one life. That life is God. That life is my life now. That life animates every organ and every function of my physical body. It circulates through me, filling me with perfect life. All the energy, all the action and all the vitality that there is is pouring through me now."

If we wish to pray affirmatively for someone else, we would say, "This life is flowing through this person now." When we pray affirmatively for others, we are recognizing God in them. We are thinking of God as being their life, their power, their strength, their vitality. We are definitely stating that this is the way it is.

If we will practice this patiently and persistently over a period of time, we will be amazed at the results. What a wonderful experiment this will be! It is perhaps the greatest adventure we will ever make. As we begin to see the signs following our spiritual communion and our affirmative belief, we will be given an assurance, a faith and a conviction such as never came to us before.

We are already familiar with the idea of psychosomatic medicine, or body-mind relationships, but now we are adding spiritual-psychosomatic medicine, or using the power, or Spirit, to direct the mind so that it will rightly control the body. This is the next step to be taken.

In doing this, we deny neither the mind nor the important place it must have in our everyday lives. But we do affirm something else: the presence of the Spirit; the realization of the divine presence in everything and through everyone; and the power of the law of Mind.

Gradually, as we reach out and begin to use this power for definite purposes, it will become as natural to affirm the divine presence when we get up in the morning as it has been to wonder what is going to happen during the day. We will feel that we are no longer alone, buffeted by fate. We have a divine companion, an infinite intelligence and an all-powerful good cooperating with us.

CHAPTER 4

EFFECTIVE PRAYER

THERE IS NO DOUBT THAT THERE IS A POWER FOR GOOD IN the universe that we can and should use. The question is, why don't we use it more effectively? If all things are possible to faith, why don't we have more faith? If affirmative prayers are answered, why don't we always pray affirmatively?

It does seem strange that we might be keeping success and happiness away from us without knowing it, since these are qualities we all desire. One of the most interesting things we can consider is the working of our mind in its relationship with the power greater than we are. Let us try to figure out just how the law of Mind works and how we can better cooperate with it.

We begin with the thought that we are all united with invisible forces that are creative. We are already one with a universal law of Mind that can do anything and one with the divine intelligence that knows all things.

The next thing for us to consider is that we are thinking and active centers in Mind, and the sum total of all our thoughts is either silently attracting our good toward us or repelling it from us.

The third proposition is that we can change our thinking and, in so doing, cause the law to act affirmatively for us instead of negatively.

We begin with the first idea, that we are surrounded by a creative law of Mind that reacts to our thought. This is the basis of all effective prayer, and this is why Jesus told us that when we pray we should believe we already have what we desire. He implied that there is a power that must react to us. He also implied that when this power reacts to us, it has no choice other than to react to us according to the way we think.

I do not think we have quite understood the significance and the full meaning of this bold claim that Jesus made. No one else has ever said it in the same way before. Up until the time of Jesus, those who preceded him said that God might help us, that there were concessions God would make if we performed certain rites or ceremonies to please God. This was good and helpful, but Jesus changed those suppositions into certainties. He said simply and directly that there is a power which operates on our belief the way we believe. But, he added, that even the law, which is all-powerful, can bring us only as much good as we accept. This accepting is an act of our own mind; it is an act of faith.

It has been only within the last hundred years or less that people have come to realize that Jesus was talking about a spiritual principle in which we all are rooted, which operates on our faith, our conviction and our acceptance. I have no doubt that within the next hundred years the world will fully accept this. But we cannot wait so long. What we should do is come to understand exactly what Jesus was talking about and realize that he meant what he said.

It is the very simplicity of his claim that causes us to overlook its deep and dynamic meaning. Jesus was really saying this: We are surrounded by a Mind, a power, intelligence or principle that receives the impress of our thought and acts on it exactly as we think. Our thought is like an object held in front of a mirror. The mirror will always reflect the object exactly. The law of Mind, like a mirror, reflects back to us what we think.

Now we come to our second proposition: We are thinking and active centers in this Mind, and the sum total of all our thought is either silently attracting our good to us or repelling it from us. This shows the part that we are to play in our use of the power greater than we are. It is the sum total of all our thinking that we must consider. In doing this, one of the first things we learn is that ninety percent of our mental activity is unconscious.

The subconscious mind is a storehouse that retains all the thoughts and memories we have ever had. It is this subconscious storehouse of memory, previous acts, thoughts and emotional reactions to life that psychologists deal with. Our success or failure, our happiness or misery is largely determined by the content of the subconscious.

Scientific investigation verifies this. Most of our thinking is unconscious. Here is where habitual patterns of thought are laid down from infancy, and the whole purpose of applied psychology is to find out what these thought patterns are and, when they are unhappy, morbid or filled with fear, change them so that the natural, normal flow of the life force will be resumed.

Of course, we have no controversy with psychologists. We follow them as far as they go. But we do add something to their philosophy, because we believe that there is a universal principle of Mind that is always reacting to our thinking, whether it is conscious or unconscious. We really are attracting or repelling the good we desire according to the whole body of our thought.

We come now to our third idea: We can change our thinking and, in so doing, cause the law of Mind to act affirmatively for us instead of negatively. It may seem astonishing, but Jesus actually gave us a technique for this, perhaps the greatest technique ever given, because he understood all these things better than we do. He implied that many of our beliefs are changed only through prayer and fasting, through meditation, and perhaps quite a bit of effort, in which of course he was right. He said that we had better pray without ceasing. He also said it would be well if our conversations were "Yes, yes" and "No, no." From what we know about the way the mind works, this was a perfect idea, because Jesus was implying that we are either affirming our good or denying it, and that both the thing we greatly fear as well as that which we have faith in can come to us.

Jesus added something else. He told us that when our faith is in the good, it will automatically obliterate evil. Good and evil are not equal powers. Good always overcomes evil. The affirmative attitude will always overcome the negative. Psychology has also proven this, and that is why many psychologists tell us to accentuate the positive and forget the negative. Continue thinking about peace and let confusion go. Affirm the good and forget the evil. This is a sound teaching.

We really are surrounded by a creative law of Mind that reacts to our thinking. The sum total of all our thinking really decides what is going to happen to us. We can actually change our thinking and cause the very law that limited us to bring us freedom.

Jesus said, "If you know these things, happy are you if

you do them." So let us proceed to the doing. Returning to our first proposition, that we are surrounded by a law of Mind that acts creatively on our thinking, let us see if we cannot make this the basis of our belief. Do we really accept that there is a self-operating power around us, a power that actually can and will do whatever ought to be done for us if we believe in it? Do we really accept that the sum total of our thinking decides what is going to happen to us?

We must believe. But since it is natural to believe and to have faith, when we find that we lack these qualities, we now know what to do about it because belief and faith are mental attitudes. So we should practice affirming daily: "I do have faith. I do have conviction. I do believe. I do know and understand that there is a power greater than I am. I do realize I can use it. There is nothing in me that can doubt, deny or limit this power. My whole being accepts it, both consciously and subconsciously." In this way we will be preparing our minds to pray affirmatively, which means to pray effectively.

This is probably the most important single thing we can do in preparing our minds to embark on the great adventure of dynamic, spiritual self-expression, because the whole basis of our thought and the whole principle of the way it acts is involved. If there is a principle of Mind that reacts to our thinking or to our belief, then it naturally follows that if we say, "It cannot," then it cannot, because we do not let it. If we say, "It will not," then it will not, because we do not permit it. If we limit it to a little good, it will not give us a greater good. The power itself is absolute; the way we use it is relative. Getting back to the words of Jesus, this is what he meant when he said that it is done to us as we believe.

The first thing is to be certain that we do believe. Science, revelation, intuition and experience teach that we may believe, and there is no reason why we should not. British scientist John Haldane said that science has only discovered one thing that is creative, and that is mind. This is why Jesus based his whole thought about God, humankind and human destiny on the simple necessity of our belief.

We can practice believing because thoughts are things. When we say, "I believe" and "There is no doubt in me," we do two things: We affirm our belief; and, by so doing, we build a positive acceptance in the mind at the same time that we reject our doubts by denying them. This is the way thought works. Realizing that ninety percent of our thinking is unconscious, we should daily affirm that there is nothing in us that denies the good we affirm, that every experience we have ever had up until now which denies our good is wiped out of our memory as a negative force, and that we are forgiven our mistakes and encouraged to go on and do better.

Now we are ready to do the work of believing that

we possess the good we desire even though we do not see any possible way for it to happen. This can be reduced to a simple method. We can say, "I do accept this good. I do believe my prayer is answered. I do affirm the presence of love, friendship, happiness, prosperity, health, peace—whatever the need may be—and nothing in me denies, rejects or refutes it. I do accept it."

After we have done this for a while, a gradual acceptance of our affirmation comes to us. We learn that as the subjective reactions of our thought build up an affirmative attitude, things begin to change in our environment. It may take a little time, but we now have courage, knowing that we are dealing with a definite principle and that it cannot fail.

Sometimes when we try to reverse our thought process, we find it a little difficult because the old negative thought patterns come to the surface and deny us the right to think affirmatively, the right to use this great, silent, invisible, creative power for definite purposes.

Sometimes when a negative thought arises, it will instantly dissolve when we say, "It isn't so. You have no power. You have no reality. You have no existence." Or, instead of denying negative thought, another method is to affirm the opposite. In this way we find the negation gradually disappears. By experimenting, we can discover how to meet the denials of life and gradually convert them into great affirmations.

This should never be done with any sense of morbidity or struggle or in any sense that we are fighting an opposing force, but rather with a calm, peaceful, inward assurance because we know what we are doing and why. We understand how the law of Mind works. We know how to use it, and we are, perhaps for the first time, applying it for definite purposes. We are experimenting, but we are experimenting with the fundamental law of our own being, the law that we believe governs everything in our life. So we are doing something not only worthwhile but something that should be very interesting.

We are all surrounded by a certain amount of skepticism and doubt, and perhaps many people think that this is all nonsense. That should not bother us in the least. We should know that we are working independently with God and the great law of cause and effect. Whether we are working for our family, our friends, the whole world or ourselves, every affirmative spiritual statement we make will have some power and an invisible law will be acting on it.

We have no one to prove this to but ourselves. We have no authority for what we do other than the authority of what happens when we do it. Jesus understood this perfectly and went about proving the supremacy of good in the midst of a world torn with confusions, even as our world is today.

We will have to do the same thing, knowing that we

have nothing to give the world unless we have first proven it. The blind cannot lead the blind. But alone with truth, one person can pass from weakness into strength, from fear into faith, from defeat into success, and from a fear of death into a consciousness of everlasting life.

CHAPTER 5

SPIRITUAL HEALING

IT HAS BEEN PROVEN THAT THE LARGER PART OF OUR physical problems is a direct or indirect result of our thinking and that we can change our thought patterns. This does not mean that physical diseases are only in our minds or that they are mental illusions. If we have pain, we know it. It will neither do us any good nor will it heal us if some thoughtless person says, "It's all in your mind." If we hurt, we know that we hurt.

I am reminded of the child who was scratching her head at the dinner table, and her mother said, "Child, why do you scratch your head?" She replied, "Because I am the only person alive who knows that it itches." This child was not a philosopher, she was not a scientist, and she did not pretend to know all the answers, but I think her reasoning was most satisfactory. She knew that her head itched, and she knew that it felt good to scratch it. And she was right.

If you or I had an allergy that irritated our skin and we went to a physician, there is a chance that the doctor would tell us that the real cause of our allergy and the physical discomfort attending it is an inward emotional disturbance of which we are not even aware. The doctor would not be saying that it is only in our mind and therefore of no importance. The doctor would merely be implying that our thoughts and emotions don't come together correctly, that there is an inward turmoil, or mental conflict, that is causing our physical trouble. Then, very likely, the doctor would suggest that we change our thoughts and feelings in such a way as to uproot the cause of our physical disturbance.

But doctors cannot compel us to think constructively. They cannot give us a pill of happiness that will remove all discontent from our mind, nor can they write out a prescription that will keep us from worrying. In modern medicine, they do not try to do this. When they feel the seat of our physical troubles lies in the emotions, they give us a sort of mental prescription that will straighten out our thinking.

But even here something will be missing unless we add some other factors that are spiritual in their nature.

No one ever worries if they have a complete sense of security, and no one ever worries if they have a complete faith. In the last analysis, all our thinking is based on our deep convictions about life. We have physical bodies and we have minds, but we are also spiritual beings and it is the Spirit within us that uses the mind, while the mind reflects or reacts on the body.

The answer to our problem, then, is not merely in saying that it is either all in the body or all in the mind. While it is true that we can establish a relationship of the mind to the body, there is a deeper truth than this and a more important one, and that is the relationship that our mind has to life itself. Our faith in life has a direct relationship to our belief in the power greater than we are that we can use. We not only have to establish a right relationship between mind and body, but it is equally important that we establish a right relationship between mind and Spirit.

A physician might tell someone with stomach ulcers that the cause of their trouble may possibly be a sense of insecurity, and the diagnosis would probably be correct. But the real and lasting cure is something else entirely. If people are suffering from a sense of insecurity, it will not do much good to point out this fact to them unless it is also pointed out that there is a kind of security that is great enough and deep-seated enough to overcome their sense of insecurity.

This is something that medicine, as such, does not pretend to touch. It merely points to the fact. The kind of security necessary to supply this need is not in a bottle or a pill, nor in any physical application or manipulation. While these are at times necessary, they are only temporary cures, and there is a great difference between being temporarily relieved of an irritation and being healed of its cause so that it cannot reappear. The physician can relieve us, but only God can heal.

We are rooted in pure Spirit, whether we know it or not. We did not have anything to do with this. We did not create ourselves. But we do seem to have pretty effectively messed up what God has made, and we seem to have this privilege. However, our roots lie in the Spirit, and in most cases what we really need is a healing of the mind even more than a healing of the body.

If it can be established that the mind produces a large proportion of our physical troubles and that changing our mental and emotional reactions to life can heal them, then we are establishing another fact that we are apt to overlook: *We have created all our mental patterns and there is nothing in the mind that has not been put there.* All our habitual patterns of thought have been unconsciously laid down over a period of many years. What we need, then, is a spiritual healing of the mind. We may have the assurance from science, from medicine and from psychology that we are not laboring under an illusion when we say that if we permit the Spirit to heal the mind, the mind will react on the body.

If a sense of insecurity—the emotion of fear and the feeling that we are inadequate to cope with life—can produce disastrous results in the body, then it becomes necessary for us to find something that will remove this feeling of insecurity and inadequacy.

No one has yet been able to supply this need out of the human mind alone, and no one will ever be able to. Just as a tree cannot live without its roots or bear fruit without drawing on the invisible source of its life, so we cannot hope to be well, whole or happy until we learn to draw on the invisible forces of the Spirit that are around us and within us.

Spirit is already perfect, and it is only reasonable that what God has made must be as perfect as God is. There is a spiritual body in which every organ, action and function of our physical being is rooted and from which it draws its life, and we should readjust our thinking to include the idea that every action of our physical body can be controlled by the Spirit within us.

This in no way denies the physical body; rather, it puts it in its right place. It does not deny the mind or the thoughts we have or the effects they have on the body. It merely puts them in their proper perspective. Beyond and above both mind and body, it introduces the idea of a spiritual person, the God-intended individual. If this

God-intended individual were not here, you and I would not be here.

We need to find the spiritual idea, the spiritual reality behind everything. For instance, we speak of people having heart trouble, but what we really mean is that these people have troubled hearts. That is, they have mental and emotional stress and strains that produce a similar effect on this vital organ.

Jesus said, "Let not your heart be troubled; you believe in God, believe also in me." When he spoke of "believing in me," he meant believing in the spiritual individual, the Christ-Spirit within us, not only the child of the living God but the living child *of* God. The spiritual equivalent that can overcome most heart trouble will have to be something that overcomes the troubled heart, the disturbed thought, the inward conflicts with life, the repressions and depressions, and the deep unconscious congestions that the mind has because it is confused, distraught, unhappy and afraid.

The spiritual equivalent of fear is faith. The spiritual equivalent of doubt is certainty. The spiritual equivalent of irritation, agitation and inflammation is peace, poise and calm. The most effective form of mental healing, the most perfect psychology, the most nearly right psychosomatic medicine is something that reaches deeper than human experience, something that reaches beyond this little world in which we live and penetrates into the divine life by which we live and without which there could be no life.

Spiritual healing is rearranging our thinking and our reactions to life so that they draw on the infinite source of all being, which is God. This is the office of prayer, of meditation and of that affirmation of faith to which Jesus said all things are possible. When spiritual mind healing is really understood, it will be practiced by everyone because it is the most natural, normal and spontaneous thing in the world.

We had to learn to acquire doubts and fears. It took us a long time to create our inner conflicts and emotional disturbances. They are truly creations of the human mind. This does not mean that they are unreal or that we can laugh them off or that we can get rid of them merely by saying they are not there. That is poor medicine from any viewpoint, and inadequate. If physicians find a deficiency in the human body, they supply the need. If psychologists find an inward emotional disturbance, they try to straighten it out. How can the picture be complete until we also discover the true relationship that the mind has to the Spirit? We will find many deficiencies in the mind that only the vitamins of faith, hope and assurance can supply.

It may take time and effort to do this. It may take the will to be well, the determination to think straight, the courage to face the immediate emergency with a calm trust and a deep and abiding faith. This is something that no one can give to us but ourselves, but we all have the power within ourselves to do this. This is what spiritual mind healing really means.

In actual practice, we take certain statements, thoughts or affirmations and meditate on them until the mind both consciously and subconsciously comes to complete agreement. Then the mind becomes calm, peaceful and no longer agitated. Then we mentally identify ourselves with the Spirit. This is why we say, "There is one life, and that life is God." But this statement is not complete until we add "and that life is my life now." This is what we mean by identifying ourselves with God, or finding ourselves in God. At first this statement may not have much effect, but daily repeating such statements and feeling their meaning inwardly can produce a transformation of one's entire life. At times this transformation is instant and permanent. But such times are rare. We need not depend on the inspiration of such a moment because the calm persistent following of this method will always produce results. None of us can change our thinking in a moment, but if we know that we are working with the great reality, then we have the courage to go on. If we gain a little every day, we are content because we know we are on the road that ultimately will lead to success.

Spiritual healing is an established fact in human experience. It follows a definite law of Mind. The pioneering work in this field has been pretty well completed and we may accept it as true and valid. What we need now is the application, and this is something that each of us may do for ourselves, perhaps better than anyone else could do for us. There are no particular formulas for doing this. It is a matter of always trying to reach back to the Spirit within us, always trying to sense its presence and its action through us, always believing that it is there, and never denying it.

How wonderful it is to realize that we have access to such a presence and such a power! How wonderful it will be when we all draw closer to this presence and power in thought, in word, and in feeling. When the day comes that the majority of people on Earth do this, a new race will walk this planet.

CHAPTER 6

THE SPIRIT INSIDE

WHILE IT IS TRUE THAT WE DO NOT ALWAYS GET ALONG with other people as well as we might, it is also certain that we could not get along without each other. We need each other more than we realize. The world is made up of people, and human relationships are merely people reacting to each other. Many businesses maintain human relations departments for the purpose of helping people appreciate each other and get along together in their work.

Psychology tells us that the two things people are interested in the most are love and personality. This is not unusual, because everyone wants to love and be loved. Everyone wants to feel needed. We all want to feel that we play an important role in life. Everyone is attracted to people with winning personalities. Thousands of books have been written on this subject, and perhaps hundreds of thousands of people have taken courses to be taught how to develop a winning personality. But those who never had the opportunity of reading these books or taking these classes would also undoubtedly like to enlarge their circle of friends and expand their influence in the activities in which they are engaged. The principle that there is a power greater than we are that is available to us is based largely on the words and works of Jesus, so it is valuable for us to find out what Jesus taught about personality.

In many ways, Jesus was the greatest individual who ever lived. Yet, there was nothing arrogant in his teaching. He taught a simple and direct approach to God and to others which, at first, looks like a false humility. We read about him facing the political, military and ecclesiastical powers of his day with calm assurance. We find him facing death with such a certainty of life that there was nothing bitter or resentful among his last words. They were merely, "Lord, forgive them, for they know not what they do" and "Lord, into your hands I commend my Spirit."

You and I are interested in the Spirit within us that Jesus was talking about. Whatever our personality may be or whatever it is to become is wrapped up in this one idea: There is a Spirit in humankind and God is incarnated in every living soul. This Spirit inside us is the gift of heaven, and without it we would not be alive. It is recognition of this Spirit with us that is the true starting point for the development of personality.

We have often patterned our lives after the lives of others. Yet Emerson told us that imitation is suicide and that all people should watch the spark of genius that flashes across their own minds and trust it. Personality, no matter how winsome, convincing or dominant it may be, is more than a mask we wear; it is a manifestation of an inner, hidden principle, a divine spark within us that uses both the mind and the body for its own self-expression.

We could think up all the beautiful things to say or the best methods of approaching people and study all the arts of personality development that have ever been taught, and still fall flat on our faces as far as the real personality is concerned. Personality is the flowering of the Spirit within us, the coming forth of a secret relationship that we have with God. Those individuals who have greatly influenced the human race throughout the ages are the ones who have known this and who have made little effort to influence others. They are the ones who have had the deepest feeling of the divine presence inside them.

We might say, "I don't wish to make a mark on history. I don't feel myself capable of becoming a great leader or a dominant factor in social, political or commercial life.

All I want is just to be happy and get along with people and have them like me." And we would be right, because the development of real personality must be something that attracts to itself everything necessary for its wellbeing, which includes love and friendship, right human relationships, success and happiness.

But those who make personal ambition their main approach to life always seem to fail. Again, we are privileged to go back to one of the fundamental thoughts of Jesus, who knew what our human needs are and never belittled them. He said that all these things will be added if we discover the real secret of life and first uncover within ourselves something that we did not even put there, something that we might call the hidden self.

No one will ever be satisfied, happy or secure in simply developing a dominant personality. Those who try to win their way through life by force eventually become weary with the struggle—a mad ambition the end and aim of which never reaches its final goal. Personality is not an external thing at all, because everything we think, say and do and everything that we appear to be outwardly is always a result of some hidden fire burning at the center of our being, some divine reality that we did not create but which we may discover. Those who find themselves in God will discover at the center of their own being something that dominates without effort, something that does not have to assume a false front, something that, by the very nature of its being, is both human and divine.

Some may say, "But now you are introducing religious ideas that we don't want to be bothered with. What we want is something that can take us into the activities of life in a triumphant manner." This is both right and wrong; right, in that we wish to be successful in living, but wrong if we think that of ourselves we can add to or take from what God already has given. While we can and should develop an outer personality, behind this there is something we never thought up. We did not plan it. We did not create it. Finding this thing is like exploring a new land that existed before we discovered it. There are heights and depths to our own being that we have not discovered.

Our personality, with all its emotions, feelings, actions and reactions, is real enough, but behind it there is something more. It is this something more that should be the starting point for the development of the personality. There is a Spirit in each individual because God is incarnated in everything. This Spirit has made each one of us just a little different in order that there may be a variation in life.

Why then should we expect any two individuals to be alike? We should not even believe that they ought to or can be identical. We should not study to be alike but rather to develop what we really are. Unity does not mean uniformity. Our unity with other people never means that we must think and act as they do. All it means is that we should get along with them. We should unify with everything while at the same time keeping intact and whole that God-given something at the center of our being, which is the real self.

It is, then, to find our true center—this divine person within us and within everyone who, in a sense, has one hand placed in the hand of God and the other outstretched to humanity—that is the end and aim of our search. Those people who find themselves in God will discover God in others. They will look through different eyes than those who think they are alone. They draw strength and inspiration from life itself, because no one can live without God and be whole.

Jesus was a dominant personality. He was the most triumphant person who ever lived because he had discovered his true nature, that part of him which was rooted in pure Spirit and revealed the strength and the power and the peace of this invisible presence that we call *God*.

Since everything is included in God—because God must be the only presence and power that there is, otherwise nothing could exist—the people who want to make the most of themselves will have to be the ones who have discovered more of themselves in that which is greater than they are. Our capacity to think, live and move, or to do anything, is nonphysical and nonmaterial. There is an invisible self hidden within us that has its source in a

higher reality and that thinks through our minds, express-
es through our actions, and reveals itself in what we are.

Since this is true, there must be at the center of our
being a divine person, a unique incarnation of God. This
is the source of all real inspiration. Here and here alone,
at the center of our being, is the real creative power. The
question is whether we are living from this center or
thinking of ourselves as detached, separate, divided, alone
and inadequate. Each of us has such a center, and we all
have direct access to the infinite presence, the universal
person. Jesus called this *the Spirit within us*, and there could
be no more beautiful thought than this, that the divine
Spirit itself, infinite as it is, is also within us.

We want to find some direct and simple approach
to this center of all inspiration and all power. Then we
want to live from it, to think and act and move from
it. This does not mean that we have to retire from the
ordinary activities of life or repress our personalities as
though they were unworthy. Quite the opposite. We
carry this vision with us into every activity. It becomes
the power behind all our actions. It appears in our relationships with others. We are more ourselves. Realizing
that this divine center within us is love, and that the same
center exists in others, we will meet people in love and
with consideration, and they will feel something flowing
from us, something that cannot be weighed or measured
or that we can say looks like this or that or something

else. It really is something that is felt but not seen.

Realizing that this divine center within us—the real person—is an individualization of the Spirit itself, we shall not be weary. Work will become play. Realizing that this center within us is pure affirmation, we will have no fear. The wonderful thing about it all is the simplicity of it, the directness. All people should take time to become acquainted with themselves, to find God in the only place they can find God, and to explore this inward, largely unknown country, the divine center in the depths of everyone's mind.

But how can we do this unless we are first convinced that it really is there? We cannot act as though something were true unless we first believe it. This is why Jesus laid such stress on the need of our believing, of our having faith, of our accepting that we are one with God. With this acceptance of God, there must come an acceptance of our real self that blossoms in our relations with others and finds fruition in its own action.

CHAPTER 7

HEAL YOURSELF

SCIENCE HAS DISCOVERED THAT SEVENTY-FIVE PERCENT OR more of our physical ailments are due to inner emotional disturbances. It has also been found that eighty-five percent of our accidents are brought about because of our inner conflicts. We know that our dealings with others mostly depend on our mental attitude. Whether we are happy, contented and have an inward sense of peace, poise and security must of necessity be a result of the way we think.

It is easy enough, then, to let these problems answer themselves. If we can be whole inside, we will not have to worry very much about what happens outwardly. When we are rightly adjusted to life, living seems to adjust itself to us.

One of our main problems is that when we are confronted with difficulties, we are prone to feel that circumstances are against us or that the trouble lies with other person and not with us. It takes well-rounded individuals to be willing to admit that they bring most of their troubles on themselves. But this is the starting point of a well-ordered life, and we may as well admit it and, if necessary, begin all over again, not trying to adjust things and people to our way of thinking, but trying to adjust our own thoughts and feelings so we will harmonize with others and fit into our environment.

In a certain, definite sense, all of us are physicians in our own minds, to our own bodies and to our own affairs. The chances are good that if we go to a modern physician for a physical diagnosis, the doctor would explain that there are certain fundamental emotional attitudes toward life that everyone must have if they expect to remain whole and healthy. If we were to go to those who have made a study of human relations and tell them that we are out of sorts with our environment, they would not try to change our environment for us, because this they could not do. They would instead show us how to adjust our own thinking to that environment, because all human relations come down to the art of getting along with others.

If we are in business and hire experts to analyze what we are doing and show us how to do it better, they might point out certain wrong adjustments, particular situations that could be corrected only by a new viewpoint. This leads us right back to the self, to that something inside us which is the arbiter of our fate, and to the way we are using certain laws in nature that govern everything.

We speak of Jesus as the great physician, the one who could point out the reason for our difficulties. If Jesus is the great physician, then it is because there were certain adjustments that he must have made to life and to living. These were the result of his communion with the Spirit. He had harmonized himself with life. He had formed a partnership with God. He had plumbed the depths of human existence and human experience and discovered that there is a spiritual reality at the center of every individual's being, a divine presence and an infinite wisdom that can and will lead, guide and direct when we let it.

We think of Jesus as the most inspired human and the greatest spiritual teacher who ever lived, and we are right. But there is something else that we may have overlooked. Jesus had a spiritual common sense and logic which history has never been able to refute and which human experience cannot deny. For instance, Jesus said, "Consider the lilies of the field, how they grow; they toil not, neither do they spin. And yet I say unto you, that even Solomon in all his glory was not arrayed like one of these." He also told us to consider the birds of the air and beasts of the field, how they live and travel about and find food and shelter by some divine direction that flows through them like blood flowing though their beings. He said, "Wherefore, if God so clothe the grass of the field...shall God not much more clothe you, O ye of little faith!"

This really is uncommon common sense, because Jesus was merely saying that there is a divine intelligence that created you. There is a divine law that governs all creation. There is a presence at the center of everything, otherwise nothing could be here. He said that if you search deep into your own nature, you will discover that this presence is within you as well as around you. It already knows why you are here and what you are and how you should act. It already knows what is best. But you are refusing to accept its guidance. Every time you deny its presence, you limit its action through you. Every time you deny its guidance, you limit your own ability to know what is best. Every time you deny its presence in others, you separate yourself from them.

The whole thing is so simple and direct, yet so immediate, so close to us that it has not seemed possible that the inspiration, power and direction we know we need are accessible to us. But when we stop to think the whole thing over and give it due consideration, we are compelled to admit that a power greater than we are governs everything and an intelligence higher than ours guides all things.

We wish to live life in its fullness, but the truth is that we mostly rush hither and thither looking for something to heal us, looking for a power to make us whole, whether it be physically, mentally or emotionally, or whether it has to do with our affairs, so that we may live successfully. We are all looking for a physician outside us.

Yet, doctors who treat us would say that they are simply making certain physical adjustments in the body that enable nature to take its own course and restore us to health. Likewise, psychiatrists would tell us that they are merely making certain adjustments in our thinking and in our emotional reactions to life that will enable nature to restore a normal balance. And all that personal relations advisers would do is to help us readjust our thinking so that we will get along better with other people.

In other words, all of these people, as good and necessary as they are and as much as we need them, will concur when they say, "We are helping you to heal yourself" or "We are helping you to get in a position so that nature, or the power greater than you are, can flow through your thought, body and actions in an unobstructed manner." They are really giving us instructions that say, "Physician, heal yourself. We will do everything we can to help you. Out of our experience, we will show you what is wrong and how you can adjust yourself to a better way of living. But of ourselves, we do not have the power of life. We cannot give life to you. We cannot give happiness to you. We cannot present you with success, for the simple reason that life has already made you these gifts. You have already inherited the power to live, but you have not ad-justed yourself to it."

If every fact of science, common sense and human experience points to the fact that we must each become our own physician, we had better accept the fact and see what we can do about it. No one really wants to be poor, unhappy or sick. There are no normal people living who do not wish to get along with others and have others like them, and I have never yet met anyone who does not wish to be happy.

In an experiment, a group of psychologists placed a feed trough just outside a heavy wire fence so that the pigs could see it, smell it and almost get their noses into it, but not quite. In a short time, the pigs became frustrated because they could not get at the food they could see and smell. The frustration became so great that when the psychologists eventually removed the wire fence, with the food finally accessible, the pigs simply lay right down beside it and made no attempt to eat. It is a funny thing to think of pigs having nervous prostration, but that is what happened.

You and I are not pigs, but the lesson still applies. We, too, have erected a wire fence, a barrier, without even knowing it, between ourselves and the source of our being. A Chinese sage once exclaimed, "O human-ity, having the power to live, why will you die?" We add to this, "O humanity, having the capacity to be happy, why will you be unhappy? Possessing the intelligence to know what to do, why do you continue in your mistakes? Having the ability to get along with others, why are you surrounded by discord?"

The pigs had lost the will to try. They had lost the ambition to make another attempt. This is what frustration is. They were stopped, and the poor animals did not have the ability to sit down like the prodigal of old and think things over.

We are different. We have the ability to analyze a situation and find a solution. But we must also have the will to do this. We must have the imagination to see how it can be done. We must have a faith to believe that when it is done, everything will be well with us.

Since there are no pills we can take which will produce happiness, since there is no medicine that can give us peace of mind, and since there is no physical manipulation that can give us faith, we must look for a different kind of medicine. We must look for it in the only place it can be found—within ourselves. We are the physician. We must heal ourselves.

We are each some part of the divine life. There is within each one of us a spark of divinity. It is this original thing within us that we must become adjusted to because all of our thoughts and actions flow from it. This is why Jesus told us that we should seek the realm of God first.

Jesus was able to heal others because he had first

healed himself. He was able to direct others because he had first received direction from the divine source within himself. He was able to tell others about the realm of God because he lived in it. The starting point, then, of our new outlook on life must be that we have direct access to an intelligence that can guide us, a life force or energy or spiritual something that can heal us, and a law of Mind that we can use. This is the starting point.

We may call this faith, hope, religion, or spiritual enlightenment—they all mean the same thing. The starting point is to recognize that we are one with God here and now, and to come to realize that there is a law of Mind that can bring about any desired result, provided it is constructive. When we were children, we had this natural belief, but as we grew up and met experiences that denied the simple faith of the child, we got further and further away from the inward center of the child until our frustrations finally accumulated and, like the pigs, we refused to even try anymore. So we have to start all over and experience some kind of a new birth, a real and actual conversion.

This has probably been the power and the vitality of every religion the world has ever known, because no matter what form each has taken they have all believed in something greater than the human. Basic religion, rightly understood, is more than a sentiment. It is more than just some happy attitude or outlook toward life. It is more fundamental than this. It is a blending of the human forces that surround us, a conscious union of the soul with its source, an *at-one-ment* with God. We all need a religion, a faith that will rekindle within us the hope that has been lost, the fire that has been extinguished, the light that has dimmed. We should not be afraid of religious convictions or look on them as weak or without meaning. A person without the hope born from faith and the conviction coming from an inward assurance is like a ship without a rudder, tossed about by wind and wave.

When we go to a physician for a diagnosis, we will follow the doctor's direction if we are intelligent. We will follow the course of treatment until we get results. The great physician, too, had a certain prescription, or instruction, that we should follow which leads back to the one central thought: Get rid of your doubts and fears. Discharge from your thought every negative attitude that denies you a right to live in harmony with life and with people. Through faith, tie your mind back to the mind of God, and in action, live as though you were guided by a supreme intelligence.

How many of us are following this divine prescription written two thousand years ago by the great physician?

CHAPTER 8

INTUITIVE WISDOM

CHILD PSYCHOLOGISTS TELL US THAT FEARS ARE ACQUIRED. What has happened to us since our infancy that has produced so many fears and uncertainties? It is the endeavor of modern psychology and psychosomatic medicine to go back into our mental and emotional life and discover the blocks, the inhibitions, the repressions and conflicts that hinder the spontaneous flow of peace, joy and creative self-expression.

A person once lived whose wisdom went way beyond our modern knowledge, and he told us that if we could keep the child in us alive, we would discover the road to peace, happiness and creativity. Jesus said that unless we become as little children, we cannot hope to enter into the realm of God. And, of course, the realm of God means a life of harmony. It means a life of peace, security and happiness. It means a life of self-expression and love, and it must mean a life filled with enthusiastic zest for living.

We must not overlook another important part of the teaching of Jesus, because he was more than an idle dreamer. He was a practical person. He told us of a spiritual power that we can use for definite purposes. One of the mistakes we have made has been to think that Jesus came to save our souls for a future state. While it is true is that he was always pointing to this future state because he knew that we are immortal beings, it is also true that he told us that we should live as though this future state is already here. He taught that there is a way of life which, while preparing us for an expansion of our being beyond the grave, also includes the expansion of our being while we are here in this world. He linked earth with heaven, time with eternity, and the now with the hereafter.

Nothing is wrong with life itself. What seems to be wrong is the way we are using it. Jesus knew what he was talking about when he said that we should relearn the simple faith and trust with which we were born, and then everything will be well with us.

Everything would be all right if we understood it. Life is for us even though we use the laws of nature wrongly. The beginning of real wisdom, the starting point of really knowing how to live, is to realize that everyone's experience emanates from themselves, while their lives emanate from God. All people have the power within themselves to reconstruct their thinking in such a manner that peace of mind, happiness, and joy in living will follow.

The simplest propositions are always the most difficult to understand, and those that are most obvious often completely elude us. We are too apt to seek roundabout methods and pathways, too apt to build up obstructions and barriers that nature has never put in our way and that really exist only in our own minds. But we can control these mental reactions because we created them. What we have made, we can unmake; what we have created, we can re-create. If God, who is the final arbiter of all human fate, has seen fit to put us here, we may be certain that it was for the purpose of expressing life to the fullest.

We may be certain that we were intended to be happy. We may be sure that everything of a discordant nature in our lives has been subsequently introduced and was never placed there by the divine will. It is all of our own creation. Not that you and I as individuals thought up or planned all the evil in the world. Rather, we suffer from a gradual accumulation of the ages.

If we can get two fundamental propositions firmly in our minds, we will find a fresh starting point. The first proposition is that God is life, God is love, and God desires only that which is right. The second is that we have obstructed the passage of divine life and love through us and led ourselves astray by a misunderstanding of the whole meaning of our relationship with God and with each other.

If we said to the average person, "Beauty is in the eye of the beholder," that person might say, "Look at all the ugliness in the world. Look at all the evil. Look at the unhappiness and confusion. How can you say that either beauty or harmony is in the eye of the beholder?" Here, we are up against a real practical proposition, and this practical proposition is ourselves. Are we able to see peace in the midst of confusion? Are we able to reach out and feel the divine presence in the midst of everything that contradicts it?

There is a story in the Bible in which an army fighting for the Lord saw the enemy, who greatly outnumbered them. Suddenly they became afraid and would have re-treated in great confusion except for a "still, small voice," the voice of the prophet of God that told them to look up. As they looked up, they saw the vast throngs fighting on their behalf. They saw a power that could completely vanquish their enemies. They felt a presence surround-ing them that would give them perfect protection. Seeing this, they were no longer afraid of the enemy, and the victory of right was gained over wrong.

This is a simple narrative, but it is not to be passed off merely as a beautiful story, because it has within it an element of deep reality—the final victory of truth over error. This is what we are confronted with in the world today. This is why it is necessary, as never before, that a great, new vision come to us, a hope and an assurance that right is might, that the power of good can vanquish its foes, and that truth crushed to earth will rise again.

Yes, beauty is in the eye of the beholder, if the beholder sees it. And peace can come out of confusion, if we listen to peace instead of confusion. This applies not only to the individual life but also to the life of the whole world, because the world itself is merely a great mass of individual lives joining their hopes and fears and aspirations in one common accord.

It is written that a nation without vision will perish from the face of the earth, and we know that an individual without a vision perishes daily. But if we can come to believe that most of our troubles are self-imposed, that they were never really intended to be, and if we can have complete conviction that there is a presence and a power that is always on the side of right, then we will have the courage to start all over again. No single individual or nation ever existed that finally won out against the power of good.

We are individuals, and we have to start with the self. Beauty, peace and joy are really in the eye of the beholder. Life belongs to the one who lives it, and gladness sings in the heart of one who is glad. We have to start with ourselves and somehow or other find our way back to the innocence, peace and joy of those days that knew no trouble, those times that had no fear because we felt the protecting presence of our human parentage. We must feel the guidance of love, wisdom, security and joy that comes only from a sense of belonging to the universe and from a feeling of trust and faith in a power greater than we are.

We had this when we were children, and then as we began the slow, tedious, and sometimes heartbreaking process of growing up, we all but lost that early vision when the world was our world, when everything was for us and nothing was against us. Whether we accept the simple proposition of Jesus, which is by far the best of all, or the slower processes of modern psychology, which painfully and laboriously take us back in our imagination to a place of security within through what it calls *self-awareness*, we will arrive at the same conclusion.

The proposition of Jesus should be accepted in all its simplicity, and those who do accept it automatically overcome the psychological and emotional barriers as if they were not there. Life is to each one of us what we make it. We will find joy if we really look for it and we will discover happiness wherever we go if we carry happiness with us.

Jesus said that we should not be too concerned about the outside of things, but "cleanse first that which is within the cup and platter." By "cup and platter," he meant our inward lives, our thoughts, our emotions, our feelings, our mental reactions to everything around, and, above everything else, our ideas about God and the destiny of our souls and the relationship we have with each other, because it is this inside of ourselves that is meant by "the eye of the beholder."

We can, without anyone's help, learn to analyze our own thinking, find out just what our reactions to life are and why, and make a real business of reeducating our minds, until finally all our reactions become positive and constructive, hopeful and helpful. But none of us do, or possibly can, live by ourselves alone.

We should start with this idea: Life is living itself in us and through us. We are a part of it. The life that entered into us has never separated itself from us; it is merely waiting for our conscious cooperation with it. Always, there is a presence with which we may commune. Always, there is a power greater than we are that we can call on. And always, God is for us, provided that we are for God. We cannot expect God to be for us if we are trying to oppose or go contrary to that which is the very essence of harmony, love, beauty and reason. But we can make up our minds to retrace our mental pathways back to the place where we started with only God, symbolized at first through our human parents and now broadened and deepened by the realization that we have not only earthly parents but also that we have a heavenly parentage.

We should retrace the pathway of our life until it leads back to the place of childlike confidence in living, and then, as it were, grow into adulthood all over again, always keeping this thought in mind: "The Spirit is daily flowing through me into action. It is daily projecting itself through me in my relations with others. The wisdom of the Spirit is guiding me. The power of the Spirit is guarding me. The presence of the Spirit goes before me and makes perfect my way."

Since we cannot live by ourselves alone, we must maintain the same attitude toward others. We must come to realize that God is incarnated in everyone. This means that the God we see in others is the same God we recognize in ourselves. If this is what we are seeing, this is what we will experience.

The person who we call the hardheaded realist might exclaim that this is just a lot of empty idealism, just a lot of wistful wishing. If so, then I would ask, "Where have you been leading us? Have you not led us to a place where the trail runs out and stops? Have you not led us up a canyon where the pathway runs into solid granite? Has your pathway led us to the mountaintops, where the perennial snows forever melt and the brooks and the rivers flow down to refresh the valleys and quench the thirst of the desert and cause the waste places to bloom and bear fruit?"

No, we are not concerned with the ideas of the hard-headed realist. Those few people to whom the world must look for inspiration were more realistic than anyone else because they discovered that for which the whole world seeks—simple peace of mind, plain joy in living and the assurance that everything is not a mistake. They have known that the power behind all things will do all things well, if we let it.

There is no question that the world will have to discover its source. There is no doubt that we must give God a chance. But to you and to me, it will forever be true that our reactions to life are in our own minds, what we see is in our own eyes, and what we experience is our own creation.

CHAPTER 9

INVISIBLE FORCES

SCIENCE SAYS THAT MOST OF US DRAW UPON ONLY TEN percent of our real capacity. The other ninety percent is submerged and goes mostly unused. It would be wonderful if we could multiply our talents ten times. I have no doubt we can do this if we really try.

It is probable that the average person would react to such a suggestion by saying, "How could it be possible that I have so much more talent than I am using? It seems too good to be true."

Let us take a simple lesson from nature. Perhaps from where you are sitting you can see a tree in full bloom. If so, remember that the tree's roots, from which it draws its life, are entirely invisible. Unless the tree drew on this invisible source, it would never flourish.

We have roots in the mind of God. Our personality, our individuality, everything that we are and do that the world sees is really a result, an effect of our invisible forces—forces that continually draw on the Infinite. But somehow or other in our ignorance we block or limit the flow of divine power into our lives.

Of course we do not do this intentionally. We all desire a pleasing personality. We want to make good in life, we want people to like us, and we desire to be worthwhile. But too often when we make an inventory of our assets, we only count and depend on the circumstances that surround us. We say, "How can I better myself? I haven't the power or the personality" or "I haven't the natural attractiveness that is necessary to make good in life." Right here is where our faith in the power greater than we are must be brought into play.

It was his great claim on God, on the power greater than he was, that enabled Jesus the human being to become a divine being while still living in the flesh.

We must come to believe that the Spirit dwells with us and that this creative Spirit, which is behind all things, flows through us. God has need of us, otherwise we would not be here. The divine power wishes to express through us, otherwise we would have no existence. As a matter of fact, we really have no existence of ourselves alone. It is only because we live in God that we live at all. If we think of ourselves as rooted in God and expect divine power to flow through us, our every act and thought will be animated by the same life, power and beauty that clothes the lily of the field. As Jesus pointed out, we would be simply following the law of our own lives.

We speak about wonderful personalities, attractive people, and people with dynamic thoughts and creative acts, and we admire them. We wonder why these people seem to be so gifted. Yet I have never known a creative person who did not realize that they were drawing on something within them that was greater than they are.

I once spoke with a popular cartoonist who had to create new ideas every day and illustrate them for a newspaper. I asked him how he accomplished so much, and he told me that he had a room with four blank walls, and the only furniture in this room was a table and a chair. When he needed ideas he would go into this room, sit down, and become quiet. When he looked around at the blank walls, there was nothing to sidetrack his attention. He would just sit there and wait for ideas to come to him.

He said that he would sometimes sit there for two or three hours and nothing would happen. Then all at once, something would begin to flow from within him—a new thought, a new idea—and he would take a pencil and begin to draw. This is the way his ideas came. His imagination drew on the invisible source within that he knew to be God. He would sit there with this mental attitude: "God is giving me ideas, and as they come to me I will draw pictures of them." Year after year, he produced. There never seemed to be any lessening of the flow, no stoppage of the creative action and no apparent limit to his ideas.

Creative artists do this, and I am sure inventors do it. Why should you and I not? We have to start with the proposition that all things are possible to God. God makes everything out of itself by the very simple process of becoming the thing God makes. There is no struggle, no holding of thoughts and no willpower involved.

We often feel that we are only half alive, but because God has implanted something within us that knows more than we do, we live in spite of ourselves. How is it that we eat a sandwich or a salad and have it turn into flesh, blood, hair and fingernails? Here is the miracle of life, the invisible becoming visible. We are so used to the process that we never question it. We just accept it; we take it for granted. Why could we not take it for granted that God will give us ideas, that the Spirit within us, as Jesus said, knows what we have need of even before we ask?

Suppose every time a tree thought of growing a new branch, it would say, "How am I going to do it? I only have a certain number of branches. I don't know how to make a new branch." Now suppose this tree is a person, just as you and I are, and it is bemoaning its fate because it would so greatly like to have a few more branches but it does not know how to make them. Thinking of the tree as a person, assume that every time the tree says, "I don't know how to make a new branch," it is blocking off the possibility of drawing its life from the soil. If this should happen, then the tree would never make any more branches. It would begin to die from that very moment.

A tree depends on nature. All that it knows is to grow, so it never short-circuits the divine energy that gives it life. But we are people, and we can short-circuit the divine energy that should be flowing through us. The irony is that we short-circuit it when we deny that it is there. The reason we deny it is because we do not see this energy. Because we do not see it, we do not believe it is there. If we really believe that all things are possible to God, then we should no longer deny that God knows what to do with God's own creation, and we should most certainly include ourselves in that creation.

What would happen to us if we included ourselves in God's creation? To start, we would learn to have a better opinion of ourselves. I am not talking about an arrogant or conceited opinion, because we have already learned that we can do nothing of ourselves. We live because we draw on the invisible source of all life. The only way that God can work for us is to work through us, and God really cannot give us anything unless we take it.

We wish to draw on this power, to let our roots run

deep into that life which is already perfect and complete. We want to live happily and without fear, because fear short-circuits the divine energy. Confusion and uncertainty cause the very power that gives us freedom to produce bondage. We should start by accepting ourselves for better or for worse. But we must be sure that we accept ourselves for better, because we are thinking of that deep, hidden self that the Bible tells us is hidden with Christ in God.

Here is where prayer and meditation make possible the miracles of life. Prayer is communion with the invisible presence that presses around us. Prayer is a reaching out and a reaching back to the divine life that sustains us. Meditation opens up an avenue in our mind for the outflow of this life. Remember, we are talking about *affirmative* prayer, because there should be nothing negative in our communion with God. It should always be affirmative. We should never say that God cannot or will not, but always that God can, will and does. As we meditate on these thoughts, we should seek to make them real until nothing in us contradicts the divine fact. We cannot doubt that we are put here to express life. Jesus said, "I am come that they might have life and that they might have it more abundantly." Jesus was no pallbearer. He was a "jubilant and a beholding soul" who knew in every moment that God was with him and for him, and he continually relied on his invisible source. Jesus, more than anyone else we know of, actually believed that a spiritual force existed, and more than anyone else he recognized its presence and accepted its power.

We have to do some work with ourselves along this line. We have to train our minds to have faith and confidence in the good, the enduring and the true. After having cleared all doubt from our consciousness, we must learn daily to affirm that all the presence and all the power—all the life that there is—is in us, for us and with us.

One more thing we should not forget to add: The higher forces of life always work constructively. When we use them constructively, there seems to be no limit to their possibility. But the moment we begin to use them destructively, they appear to block themselves. This seems to be the only condition that the Divine has laid down which might be considered limiting. But it really is not limiting at all. We could not expect to use the law of Mind for evil purposes, nor could we expect to generate love through hate. Neither could we hope for God to give us that which we refuse to pass on to others. These are the only conditions Jesus laid down when he told us that we would always receive if we would pray properly.

For example, we can love without limit. We can love everyone and everything and feel kindly disposed toward people, circumstances and situations, and this attitude toward life will never hurt us. It will never dampen our ardor or enthusiasm nor will it block the flow of life through us. Rather, it will tend to accelerate it. But the moment we begin to hate, dislike or oppose, we discover that we are blocking the flow of life, and gradually these negative attitudes stifle us. They short-circuit the flow of the energy from the roots of our being into the things we are doing.

It is interesting to realize that when we are on the right track, there is no limit, but when we get on the wrong track, it runs out, stops, and we are blocked. It seems as though God has imparted God's own life to us, placing no limitation or condition that would restrict other than this: Our life must be lived constructively, in unity, love and sympathy with everything around us if we expect to live it to the fullest. I believe that every person is born to be creative, to live to the fullest and enjoy life, to be happy, glad, prosperous and whole, because I do not believe that God is a failure. No, God never makes mistakes. We are the ones who err.

If we are certain that our lives are constructive, and if our whole desire is to live in such a way as to harm no one, but to bless all, then we should place no limit on the possibilities of our future. Since everyone is an individual, we cannot rob anyone by living as though we are whole, happy and unafraid. There is nothing to be afraid of in God's world, because whether we are here or somewhere else we can be certain that God does all things well.

This great gift of life is to be accepted, even as the lilies of the field and birds of the air. Try this simple experiment by daily saying to yourself, "All that the Spirit has is mine. God wants me to be whole, happy, well and prosperous. There is nothing in me that can deny God's presence, God's power, God's wisdom, God's guidance and God's protecting love. Therefore, today and every day, I will live life to the fullest. I will sing, dance and be glad. And always within me, there is the presence and the power—the life of God. And so it is."

CHAPTER 10

SUCCESSFUL LIVING

EVERYONE WANTS TO BE A SUCCESS IN LIFE, BUT REAL success means more than just having a permanent position in society, in the commercial world or in any other one walk of life. Real success means happiness and fulfillment in everything we do, and it must include enough of "this world's good" so that we have a sense of security and wellbeing.

All these things are contained in the teachings of Jesus. He said, "Your Creator knows that you have need of these things."

Jesus did not say that God has prepared a realm for us in some future state. He told us that if we live rightly, every good thing necessary to happiness while we are on earth will be supplied, and, as a fitting climax, we will also inherit the realm of God hereafter.

But Jesus said more than this. He said the realm we will inherit is already here and that we may as well begin enjoying it today. This is why he said that we need not take anxious thought for tomorrow but that we should have such a deep and abiding trust in the power greater than we are that everything we need today will be supplied.

Jesus healed the sick because he knew this was their first need. He fed the multitudes when they were hungry and he fed them with the kind of food that sustains physical life. He did not overlook the need we all have for pleasurable living. When the wine ran out at the wedding feast, Jesus turned water into wine. In no place do we ever find Jesus separating life from living. What he did was to make heaven and earth come together and meet in our present experience. He said that the love and abundance of God's realm is at hand. Stretch forth your sickle and reap the harvest of God's abundance. Permit God to heal you of your disease. Permit God to provide everything that you need, because nothing is withheld.

How could it be otherwise? God is the great giver. Life comes fresh and new to us every day, as though it were saying, "Behold, I have laid the gifts of heaven before you." What are you going to do with them? Do you wish to remain sad and depressed in the midst of an eternal joy? You have the choice.

Jesus also told us that we must some day discover that the old forever passes into the new. He told us that we should use everything that we have to the fullest and not bury our talents in the ground or hide them; otherwise, they will become moth-eaten and rust away into nothing. It is as though he had said that life is a game. Life is continual movement. Life is forever changing. But through it all, we learn the secret of living. There is an all-sustaining law of Mind on which we may rely. There is a divine presence with which we may commune. There is a realm of peace into which we may enter. There is a joy that may be ours if we live, think and act as though we were in partnership with God right now.

It is this partnership with the Infinite that we wish to establish. We want to tune into the divine harmony so much that all discord will disappear. We want to so unify ourselves with the peace of God so that all confusion will leave us. Jesus put the whole thing together and said, in effect, "Just think it over."

If we wish people to like us, we must first like them. This takes us back to the old nursery rhyme:

"'Why does the lamb love Mary so?'
The eager children cry.
'Why, Mary loves the lamb, you know,'
The teacher did reply."

It is interesting that an old nursery rhyme teaches us about the mystery of the realm of God. We have to love if we want to be loved.

We want happiness, because there is no success without it. But happiness is a state of mind. If we want to be attracted to happy situations and happy people, we must learn to be radiant within ourselves. The law of Mind works automatically on our thoughts, and those who continually tune into unhappiness will find themselves surrounded by unhappiness, thinking that fate is against them. They must reverse their whole process of thinking, and then the miracle takes place. They gradually discover that they are living with happy people because they have become happy themselves.

We want success. If we want an intelligence greater than ours to run our business, then we must believe that there is such an intelligence and act and think as though it is actually operating in our affairs, and definitely affirm that it is, believing.

Do we need money or some other material thing necessary to our wellbeing? Jesus never condemned this. He said, "Render unto Caesar the things that are Caesar's and unto God the things that are God's." Moreover, he implied that when we have rendered unto God the things that are God's, Caesar will be taken care of. First things first. That is all he was talking about. The greater includes the lesser.

When we are confronted with pressing needs, it is not always easy to get away from the thought long enough actually to believe that those needs are met. Yet, every such condition that confronts us is but another opportunity to prove the supremacy of the Spirit and the availability of the law. We want to live more fully, and we feel that we should, because something within knows the fullness of life. We want to live more completely, and something within us knows that love is the great reality. So in our prayers and meditations, in our affirmations and denials, we must shift the whole basis of our thinking until the negative reactions no longer rise up in our thought.

As we learn to think in an affirmative manner, we find that the subconscious content of negation gradually slips away and the day comes when it is no longer there. It is then that the winds of God blow clear from the realm of heaven on earth and fill the sails of our hope with a power that takes us into the haven of our desire.

CHAPTER 11

GOD MEETS YOUR NEEDS

WE CANNOT COERCE GOD, NOR CAN WE MISUSE THE LAWS of nature. It is true that the laws of nature obey us when we first obey them. All our inner conflicts are a result of a violation of the natural laws of self-expression. No patient ever came to a psychologist or a physician whose illness did not arise out of a violation of a natural law at some point. This is why we say that disease is unnatural, whether it is a physical, emotional or mental one.

As a matter of fact, all that physicians of the mind or body do, and all that they attempt to do, is to assist in restoring the natural function of a natural law. All that physicians hope to do is to help nature do what it would do anyway if it were let alone.

It would be false to say that nature does not wish to keep us well, whole and happy, or that it is testing us to see how much we can take from life. If we followed this procedure in scientific research, we would get nowhere because the scientist always starts with the idea that there is much more freedom in nature than we have understood, and that when we comply with nature's laws we will be liberated from a bondage that nature itself never really imposed on us, but that was imposed on us by our own ignorance.

It was not too long ago that the vast Imperial Valley in California was a wasteland, a desert. We did not think it wrong to build dams and change watercourses, or even seed the clouds and cause them to give us rain. And see the result! The desert was made to blossom and bear fruit.

Here is something we should not overlook: God had already provided everything necessary to produce the abundant crops we now enjoy. Just as soon as we complied with the laws of God, which are the laws of nature, the miracle took place. We did not feel that God was testing us or trying to keep us in a state of semi-starvation because the desert had not yielded the harvest until we cultivated it. We took it for granted that it was part of the entire, divine scheme of things that when we did our part, nature would do the rest.

God does it when we let God do it. But first we have to learn how to put everything together in the right way.

As a matter of fact, when we put things together rightly, everything else is automatic. The only difference between people of ancient times and people of today is that we have learned how better to cooperate with nature.

But there are other desert places in our experience. Too often, we are unhappy or mentally un-whole. Too often, we lack the good things of life. It does not go too far to say that, too often, we are burdened with physical diseases that need never have been. The law of Mind is just as real as other laws in nature, so we should find out how it works and learn to comply with it, with the definite end in view that we shall live a fuller and happier life.

Before we can use this law, we must believe that it really exists and that we are supposed to use it. We should not think of the law of Mind as something beyond the realm of nature, as something apart from the whole scheme of things. Often, in our sincere desire to do right and be right, we are afraid to introduce the thought that we are really rooted in pure Spirit and can actually draw on divine power and use it for definite purposes.

We have too often limited ourselves by thinking that nature's laws extend only as far as we can see. Always, the laws of nature have existed universally if they have existed any place. We could not say that our horizon is the end of space just because that is as far as we can see. There are unlimited horizons, and as we begin to move toward our present horizon we discover it moves back, and it keeps moving back as we go forward. What we all need is the courage to keep moving into new horizons.

We are only beginning to learn that the laws of the universe are real, dynamic and creative, and that they can be used for definite purposes. We have found that faith is a key to the greater possibility. We have come to realize that faith acts like a law. Jesus did not break the laws of nature or God when he used faith. He merely complied with the higher law of his being. He did not deny that the paralyzed needed to be healed; he used his faith to heal them. He did not say that the multitude was not hungry; instead, he fed them. He did not say that taxes should not be paid to Caesar; he found the money with which to pay the tax. He could not have used his faith as he did if he had not been completely convinced that it was natural and right that God should help us. If we were as sure of our position as he was of his, we could then expect to receive the same answers.

The question naturally arises: Why are we not sure of our position? The answer is simple enough. We have not yet learned to try our faith. We have not experimented with it enough. We have not prepared our minds to accept the simple proposition that not only are all things possible to God, but it is also possible for us to cultivate the faith that a divine power can and will meet our human needs. The apostle Paul boldly proclaimed, "Our faith should not stand in the wisdom of humanity, but in the power of God."

Right now we are in this position. We do believe in a power greater than we are, and we do believe that it is ready and willing to meet our needs. We are just now beginning to learn how to use this power. We are beginning to understand the relationship of this power to our belief and our faith. We are beginning to understand that the way we believe and the faith we use are actually our individual way of using this power.

This is not a new idea at all. Thousands of years ago it was said that "as you think in your heart, so you are." But we have been walking through the maze of human opinions for so long that our outlook has shrunk to comply with the wisdom of people and not with the power of God.

The adventure of faith in which we are now engaged is a reopening of the horizon of the power of God. We are beginning to accept the idea and to use it by believing certain things in certain ways to get certain results. This is why even though individuals might be afflicted with some physical condition or illness, we direct them to reach beyond the present condition and believe in perfect health. And not only to believe in perfect health in general, but to believe in it for themselves.

Our belief is what directs the power of the law of Mind, but we do not acquire these beliefs by accident.

Each and every belief has been formed by previous experience until it has become a habit of thought. Because this is true, we see the possibility of changing our old beliefs and forming new ones, until they too become habits of thought. This is what we mean by scientific prayer and affirmative meditation. Of course, our prayers and meditations do not change the divine nature. They merely put us in a position to express it affirmatively. They make us obedient to the divine law so that we may use it in everything we do.

We want to know how to use this law of Mind and what might be obstructing its affirmative operation through us. When doing this, the first obstacle we come up against is the habit of thought that we have entertained for years, thought that denies the possibility of the good we wish to experience, as though something arises from our minds that says, "It's too good to be true" or "Nothing good could happen to me" or "I don't understand how to use this law anyway" or "I am not good enough to use it."

The Bible says that our enemies will be those of our own households. This is a blessing in disguise, because if our real enemies are our own thoughts, at least we have located them. We now know what they are and how they work, and we know that we can change them.

Our fear can be converted into faith, and the misuse of the law of Mind that has produced bondage can just as easily bring about our freedom. We must know that it not only can but it will, because it must. The first thing we have to do, then, is convert every negative mental attitude into a positive one, every fear into a faith, and every uncertainty into an assurance. The ones who do this best are those who have the deepest conviction and the simple, childlike belief in a power greater than they are.

Early pioneers realized that if they could get water in the desert, it would bloom. What they had to seek out were the sources from which the water flowed—the deep subterranean passages, the high mountaintops, the clouds that floated over them, and the great will of nature to create.

We can take this same idea and apply it to our mental and spiritual lives, realizing that nothing can oppose us but our own belief. We must carefully watch our thoughts and listen to the way our minds are working. When we do this, we will be surprised at the negative statements we are making about ourselves, other people, and the possibilities of life. We will be surprised how many times we deny our good every hour of the day. We will be equally surprised how easily the law works for us after converting our negative attitudes into positive ones.

In actual practice, we take a few simple statements every day and think about them until they become real to us. For instance, we might wake up in the morning saying, "This is the day that God has made, and I am going to be glad in it." Later in the day, though, we may suddenly think, "Well, I haven't very much reason to be glad. Just think of all the bad things that happened yesterday." Right here is where we must be on the alert and say, "Yesterday is gone forever. This is a new day."

If we do this, we soon discover that when a negative thought rises in our mind, we can remove its power by flatly denying it. When we affirm its exact opposite, we not only build up a resistance to the negative thought but we actually convert it into a positive power. Fear and faith are merely two ways of thinking. Each uses the same power. So we are not fighting an adversary. We are rearranging our thinking. If the thought comes that says, "What reason have I to suppose I can be happy and whole today?" we must tie our thought right back to the idea that we are one with God, one with all the life, presence and power there is, and one with the only law there is, and then affirm that God in us is happy.

God will help us. Like Jesus, we too should believe that it is the Spirit's good pleasure to give us the many blessings of the realm of heaven, remembering that life gives us our blessings through our beliefs and through our thoughts. Thus, we become diligent about the kind of thoughts we think. We are careful to see that the thoughts that flow into our consciousness are thoughts that are like our highest concept of good—thoughts of health, beauty and peace. Thoughts of life. These are thoughts about the realm of God, and it is the law of this realm alone that can free us from all our fears and set us safe on the pathway to a new life.

CHAPTER 12

COMPLETE ACCEPTANCE

BECAUSE WE ARE HUMAN, WE ALL GET THE FEELING AT TIMES that our burden is too great to bear, that the load of life is too heavy to carry. At these times, we would be grateful to discover the secret of lifting the burden and placing it on the shoulders of the power that knows no burdens.

At first, it would seem as though this means an escape from living, as though we might be running away from our problems rather than solving them. This is the last thing we should attempt to do, because we do not have to deny the reality of problems in order to find their solutions. The greater the problem, the more complete should be its answer. And the greater the burden, the more certain we should be that it can be dissolved.

The Bible clearly states that we should cast our burdens on the Lord, and that we should believe with our whole being, with everything that is within us, that there is a power that can convert these burdens into freedom and turn our fear into faith and our doubt into certainty. Jesus said, "Come unto me, all you that labor and are heavy laden, and I will give you rest." Shortly after that, Jesus departed from this world, telling his followers that he would send "the Comforter...even the Spirit of truth which proceeds from the Creator."

It seems as though Jesus were saying, "Watch carefully what I am doing and realize that I am placing my whole reliance on the Creator within me. And when I have gone away, when I have left this world, you are to realize that this Creator also dwells in you. If you accept this power, it will work for you, and your yoke will be easy and your burden will be light."

Jesus knew that he would not remain with his followers forever. He knew that all people must discover for themselves that they as individuals have a direct relationship to the Spirit. It was this Spirit, this divine Comforter, which he said would remain with us forever.

This is what is meant by relying on a power greater than we are. We are not only operated on by physical forces in the physical universe, we are also operated on by spiritual forces in the spiritual universe. Since the Spirit controls everything, including our physical bodies and affairs, Jesus told us that our first approach should be to the Spirit: "Seek first the realm of God, and all these things will be added unto you."

Jesus did not say that when we seek the realm of God, everything else will be subtracted. He said it will be added. He knew that we need physical things in a physical universe. But another thing he knew which we have not quite understood is that the spiritual can control the physical. There are no burdens in the Spirit. There is no sorrow, no grief, no sickness, no despair, no poverty, and no unhappiness in God.

It was because Jesus was so consciously aware of the divine presence and the operation of the law in everything he did, and because he so definitely drew upon it, that he was able to do what he did. He proved the power of the Spirit over all apparent resistance. He never denied the things we need. He merely affirmed that they will be provided if we join ourselves with the spiritual cause of everything. This is why he said that his yoke was easy and his burden was light. He had cast all burdens onto the Spirit. Before he did this, he must have come to a complete acceptance, a place of such absolute faith, that physical obstructions, no matter of what their nature, had no existence for him.

If Jesus had done all this and had said, "I have a power that no one else can possess," he would still have been the greatest person who ever lived. But he did not say this.

He said, "Because I have done this, you can do it also. The presence that is around and within me is around and within you. The power that is with me is with you. The law that I am using, you can use."

He carefully told us exactly what to do to remove every obstruction from the pathway of wholeness: Give, and to you will be given. Love, and you will be loved. Enter into peace, and you will become peaceful. Find the joy that I have found, and you will be joyful. Arrive at the faith at which I have arrived, and you will "know the truth, and the truth will make you free." Get rid of the burdens of your own mind. Get everything out of your thinking that is afraid or that doubts or is uncertain, and then you will find that you already have entered into the realm that is forever at hand and within you.

This is the key to the whole situation. You and I have burdens, but God has none. You and I have fears, doubts, uncertainties and worries. God has none of these things. They do not belong to the divine realm, not if Jesus knew what he was talking about. Jesus prayed that this realm of God should come on earth even as it is in heaven, and then he said it will come to us as individuals and to the world as a whole when you and I and the world rightly interpret life.

When casting off our burdens, we must rid ourselves of our negative thoughts and feelings, our doubts and uncertainties, our unhappiness and despair. We have nothing to offer God other than our simple and sincere acceptance. God cannot give us what we need until we first remove the obstructions in our own minds. In a certain sense, life has already given us everything. But nothing is ours until we use it, and even the Divine must wait on our acceptance.

Let us see how this works in actual experience. Suppose we are confused and lack peace of mind. There are so many reasons why we are confused, so many reasons why it is impossible to have peace of mind. There is so much that we have to do, so many things we have to attend to, so much unfinished business. We think we are too busy to get still, to become quiet and listen to peace. This is a mistake. No one is too busy to be made whole.

Peace already exists at the innermost center of everything. As we become quiet and meditate on peace, if thoughts come up in the mind that argue against our being peaceful, these are the burdens that we must release. When the thought comes that says there is so much confusion in the world, it becomes impossible for us to become peaceful. We should then say, "That is a lie about the truth. The truth is that peace exists. I will no longer listen to the confusion. I am listening to peace."

If we do this only for a few moments, we will discover that peace seems to envelop us and flow through us. The confusion actually disappears because we have cast our burden of confusion on the law, which knows no confusion. It is as though we throw a snowball in a pail of boiling water and watch it dissolve. The water does not argue against the snowball, and the snowball cannot resist the heat of the water. It has no choice other than to melt and become a part of the water. So it is with our fear if we can get still long enough to have faith. The fear then becomes subject to something greater than it is, an all-powerful and unconquerable force, which dissolves it until finally the fear itself is converted into positive faith.

I am certainly not denying that we have burdens. I am simply saying that there is something that has no burdens, there is something that knows no confusion, and there is something that has no fear. That something is already right where we are. Emerson said that we are surrounded by spiritual laws that execute themselves, and added, "For it is only the finite that has wrought and suffered; the infinite lies stretched in smiling repose." All great spiritual geniuses have understood this.

Our trouble is not with reality or with the truth. It is with us—our confusions, our doubts, our fears. We will have to convert these, and it may take time and patience. But how far have we come by adding confusion to confusion, fear to fear, doubt to uncertainty, and misery to unhappiness? We do not extinguish a fire by throwing on more fuel.

There is no use for us to wait for things to become better in our outside world, no use to wait for some terrific experience to come to us that will make everything right, no use to wait at all. The place to begin is right where we are, and the time to start is now. The power already exists, the law is already operating, and the divine presence has never left us. God is still in heaven, and God's realm is already within us.

I believe that we are surrounded by a spiritual law that executes itself. I have no doubt at all that Jesus understood this perfectly and used it completely. Nor do I have the slightest doubt that we can use it. Perhaps we are using it now in reverse. Perhaps the very faith we have in our fear causes the thing we fear to come into our experience. Perhaps all we have to do is to reverse this process in our own thinking.

It seems to me that this is true and that we are not really dealing with good and evil but only with one power that we can use in two ways. But it is a power that finally delivers itself to us completely only when we use it for good and constructive purposes. If we can simply come to feel that nothing is really against us and everything is for us ("If God be for us, who can be against us?"), this would be the supreme affirmation, the complete abandonment of our faith to spiritual law.

This is the experiment on which you and I are embarked. This is the thing we wish to prove above everything else. This is the great lesson that the world needs, so we should enter into this experiment with joy.

We should have a great surge of thankfulness, and we should have a complete and childlike trust and faith. Such trust has never been misplaced. Such faith has never been denied.

CHAPTER 13

THE ETERNAL SEARCH

EVERYONE'S SEARCH IS FOR GOD BECAUSE WE ARE ALL searching for something that will make us whole. But not all of us know, or quite realize, that we really are searching for God. We have separated religion from everyday life. We have tried to separate life from living and God from nature. God is that invisible presence in the universe, the divine power that animates everything, and the law of Mind that controls everything. But we have come to feel that the realm of God is not really at hand, but that it is to transpire in a dim and unknown future.

This was not the attitude Jesus took when he proclaimed that the realm of God really is at hand, when he told us that if we would find God in ourselves, in each other, and in nature, we would find happiness and completion. We would find what the human heart not only longs for but absolutely needs, particularly in these times of stress and strain when the question arises from countless thousands: What is it all about? Why this confusion and uncertainty and fear and doubt?

Out of this great confusion will come an equally great certainty, and out of all this doubt will grow a faith. It surely will if enough people turn to that divine source from which everything springs. God really is the object of our search since divine power alone can make us whole.

Now as never before in human history we need God. We need to enter into a close communion with the living Spirit and feel the warm embrace of its eternal presence around us. We need to know that we are not pawns on a checkerboard of chance, that there is a real and deep meaning to existence, a meaning that includes this life and everything in it, and after this a life to which we may look forward with happy anticipation. Nothing less than this can give us happiness and peace.

The singer wishes to sing. The dancer wishes to dance. The individual engaged in business wishes to be a success. The individual with a family wishes to provide for them and be happy with them. Self-expression is not selfishness. Selfishness is in seeking our individual good at the expense of others. Self-expression means that we live with others in happiness, giving to them the privilege of expressing every talent they possess and rejoicing with them in their successes.

There is nothing wrong with self-expression. Life has entered into each of us in an individual way, animating everything we do and always urging us to greater things, as though there were no limit to the expansion of the individual life. We are so constituted that the greatest self-expression includes our relationship with others and our relationship with everything in life.

Jesus told us that if we find God, we will find all these things, because all these things are added to the great discovery. Jesus made heaven and earth come together. He did not say that there is a heaven that God has provided for us in a life after this life. He said that heaven is present with us. He said to the one who died with him, "Today you shall be with me in paradise." Jesus said that the realm of God is at hand and that everyone who comes into this realm through a right relationship with God will find love, friendship, success and happiness, here and now. Jesus never condemned the personal desire we all have to live happily and successfully.

The search for God is not the search for some abstract principle or some future state of being. Our search is to find that thing right where we are, to discover that thing in each other and in nature. The psalmist said that the earth is filled with the glory of God, and we all know that the great teaching of Mahatma Gandhi was not that we should renounce the world. It was that we should find God in the world. It is this finding of God in everything we do and in every person and everything we contact that is our real search.

The interesting thing we discover when we read history is that the great examples of the human race have been those who have found something that can give us the assurance that all is well, that behind the fear and doubt and uncertainty of life there is a great assurance, that at the center of the storm there is a place of peace, at the center of every person we can find God. The search is both an individual and a collective one. But, as always, we must start with the individual, and that individual means you and it means me.

Have you and I actually and persistently tried to find God in each other? I am afraid we have not. There is no use blaming ourselves. It does us no good to beat our breast and exclaim how unworthy we are. This merely adds more confusion to an already disturbed mind. Those who search after God must learn to forgive themselves and everyone else, to forget even their own weaknesses as they seek strength. They must forget their confusion and meditate on peace, and as they do this they discover that the confusion disappears. They may be sure of this. They will have to find God in themselves before they can discover God in others. This is why Jesus said that the blind cannot lead the blind. There must be a seeing eye.

When John the Baptist was asked, "What shall I do to avoid the wrath to come?" Jesus answered something like this: "My friend, I have not come to tell you how to avoid some future wrath that is to be visited on you. I have come proclaiming that the realm of God is already at hand."

This is the attitude we should take. Life holds nothing against us. It desires only our good. It wants us to be well, happy, and successful, but it wants us to play the game of life the way it is supposed to be played—in unity and cooperation with others.

These are the only rules that life has laid down for us. It has not demanded that we do something that is impossible. It has not told us that we have to understand something that only a few great intellects can comprehend. It has not even told us that we all have to become saints before we can enter into the realm of heaven. It has merely said, "Here I am. I am truth. I am wisdom. I am love. I am peace, and I am eternal goodness. Accept me!"

Suppose, then, that you and I start all over, beginning right now, and let us see if we can learn to forget all the heartache, sorrow, and pain, all the fear, frustration, and uncertainty, and go back inside ourselves until we find that little child who is not afraid because, by some divine instinct within, this child knows that "underneath are the everlasting arms."

Are we afraid of becoming that spontaneous child

again in case someone thinks we are foolish? Well, who is there among us who would not again be happy as a child? Who is there among us who would not recapture the dream of youth? No, if the greatest person who ever lived has told us that we must become as little children, we do not need to be afraid of becoming childlike.

Remember, being childlike does not imply being childish, silly or foolish. Rather, it implies the attitude scientists must have as they stand in awe before the majesty and might of the laws of nature. It is the wonder that great mathematicians must have as they contemplate the infinity of numbers. It is the reaching out toward the essence of beauty that great artists feel when they capture the glory of a sunset or the soft, radiant pathway of the moon across the water. We do not need to be afraid of being childlike. Rather, we should fear *not* being childlike, because only through an attitude of faith and trust in the universe can we ever hope to recapture our lost paradise.

If our search for God happily results in our finding God, everyone around us will soon discover this fact. If our search for happiness makes us happy without robbing others, everyone we contact will be exposed to this happiness. It will become contagious. If our search is for love, and we find it, we will become lovable, and those around us will love us because we have first loved them. If our search for security finally leads us to the place where we are no longer afraid, everyone who contacts us will be lifted up because of our faith. They will be strengthened because of our strength and they will feel secure in our security.

We must try to find God in ourselves and in each other and not be afraid to look for God in human events. Just as surely as we do this, we will find God. "Ask, and it shall be given you; seek, and you shall find; knock, and it shall be opened unto you."

The End

ERNEST SHURTLEFF HOLMES (1887–1960), an ordained Divine Science minister, was founder of a spiritual movement known as Religious Science, a part of the New Thought movement, whose spiritual philosophy is known as Science of Mind. He was the author of *The Science of Mind, Life Is What You Make It,* and numerous other metaphysical books, as well as founder of *Science of Mind* magazine, in continuous publication since 1927.

NEWT LIST is the foremost publisher of updated editions of spiritual classic texts. Newt List titles are edited to provide contemporary language structure and idioms that have evolved since the original manuscript was published. We revise punctuation and capitalizations, and adjust sentence structure when appropriate, as well as update certain words or terms that have since become obscure, as long as those changes do not affect the author's intention or meaning. More valuable for readers today, though, is Newt List's procedure of changing of gender forms. In the time of original publication, these classic books generally used masculine forms when referring to God or humankind. Newt List updates all its books using gender-neutral language, making the ideas in them apply more broadly to all readers.

newt
LIST
NewtList.com